EMOTIONAL INTELLIGENCE WORKBOOK

By Dr. Paul L. Gerhardt

CONTENTS

Emotional Intelligence in Practice

What is Emotional Intelligence and Why it is Important to Have it?

Emotional intelligence (EI or EQ), in its most concise and simplest form, may be described as the ability to recognize, evaluate and handle one's emotions along with those of others. Success today depends on a person's ability to interpret the signals from other people and react accordingly. Thus, it is advantageous for people to develop emotional intelligence skills that will enable them to understand, identify with, and negotiate with others.

There are five major classifications of emotional intelligence skills and they are:

Self-Awareness. Key to EQ is a person's ability to recognize emotions. In order to develop self-awareness, one needs to be tuned into his or her real feelings. When one is able to evaluate emotions, then those emotions can be managed. Self-awareness has the following elements:

Emotional awareness – ability to identify one's own emotions and the effects of those emotions

Self-confidence – one's confidence about his or her capabilities and self-worth

Self-regulation. A person often has little control over when an emotion is experienced. But, a person can control the length of time an emotion lasts by making use of techniques in alleviating negative emotions like depression, anger, or anxiety. Self-regulation includes:

Self-control

Trustworthiness

Conscientiousness

Adaptability

Innovation

Motivation. Being able to motivate oneself for an achievement means having a positive attitude and clear goals. Elements of motivation are:

Inner Drive for Achievement

Commitment

Optimism

Initiative

Empathy. This is the ability to identify how people are feeling. The better a person is about recognizing other people's feelings, the better that person is at being able to control the signals that he or she sends. Someone who is empathic is very good with:

Developing others

Leveraging diversity

Service orientation

Understanding others

Political awareness

Social Skills. Social skills are considered as "people skills". They are very important as a person who is able to understand, negotiate and empathize with other people is one with high emotional intelligence. The most useful social skills are:

Communication skills

Persuasion skills

Conflict management

Leadership skills

Cooperation and collaboration

Building relationships

By developing one's emotional intelligence one can become, not only more productive, but also more successful. Also one can help others to become successful and productive too. The outcomes and process of EI development contains several elements that are known to be able to reduce stress for individuals, thus, for organizations through promoting greater understanding; moderating conflicts; and fostering harmony.

In the workplace, the interactions between employees and their leaders are keys to creating a more favorable working environment. Such interactions are routinely affected by discrete intrapersonal and interpersonal skills by leaders. People with high EI have the opportunity to affect, positively, and improve the quality of both interpersonal and intrapersonal interactions.

One can develop their EI by gaining self-awareness and being able to identify his or her challenge areas and building the skills within those areas through training. EI is able to help predict success as it reflects how one is able to apply knowledge to an existing situation.

There are many researchers who have studied workplace aggression and they focused on the personality differences, as well as situational differences as precursors for their occurrence. There have also been researchers who have decided to pursue a different route and concentrate on emotional intelligence (EI) as a construct that may influence workplace outcomes in most cases.

It has been suggested that emotional intelligence (EI) may be as significant as traditional intelligence when it comes to predicting success in the workplace. It has been established that emotional intelligence is a separate construct apart from personality factors. Though many have contended that EI is actually a personality characteristic, it has been stated that the main element of EI is the general ability to identify emotions which makes it different from other personality factors.

There have been many bold statements regarding the importance of emotional intelligence which have had skeptics who insist that emotional intelligence has minimal or a modest impact, at best, in the workplace. However, despite criticism, the research in emotional intelligence has grown steadily with more researchers studying its impact in workplace effectiveness, workplace aggression and occupational stress.

There are two approaches to the study of EI. There is the study that stated that emotional intelligence describes, exclusively, abilities and used tests of performance like the Mayer-Salovey-Caruso Emotional Intelligence Test (MSCEIT) as a means to measure it. The second, states that emotional intelligence need to be studies as a trait. Both approaches proposed that emotional intelligence abilities comprises of some level of skill in the realm that is affective, along with the skill in whichever cognitive fundamentals also enmeshed in each ability. The use of self-reported tests has been suggested, like the On Emotional Quotient Inventory. The two approaches do not contradict each other in any way however they offer differing perspectives on the nature, as a construct, of emotional intelligence.

Though there are some researchers who do not consider emotional intelligence as something that affects the workplace, there are many who do and they have made many studies that support their stance. There has even been a study that suggested that there is a direct link between academic achievement and EI.

Aside from several studies that have attempted to link workplace success to emotional intelligence with empirical data which showed that EI was just as crucial, if not more, than just IQ for success in the workplace. Other than a study that has been conducted to show a direct connection between success in the workplace and EI, there is a study that has taken bold step towards showing that emotional intelligence needs to be taken as seriously as intelligence quotient (IQ) in the work environment. In that study, researchers have compared the influences of IQ and EI to performance in the workplace. Researchers found that EI was responsible for about 36 percent of total variance in the organization's success while IQ accounted for about 27 percent. It clearly showed that EI is more crucial, than IQ, to workplace performance.

In order to comprehend the idea of emotional intelligence, it is best to explore two elements: emotion and intelligence. Research that has been done on emotions and elements that are related to expressions of emotions can be traced back to over a century. Among the conventional psychological research, there is one that has defined emotions as mental activity interruptions and as a whole an disturbance of a person taking the form of a response that is disorganized, mostly visceral, which results from the deficiency of effective adjustment.

It has been asserted that emotions are considered as distractions to logical thinking and it has been proposed that any tests that are meant for measuring IQ would be best not to include questions that demonstrated grief, anger, fear, or other forms of emotional stimuli. However, the disorientation theory of emotions have been contradicted by researchers who hold the view that emotions are reactions to the version of reasoning activities and are organized responses. There is also an argument that the categorization of emotions as confused mental state and it is believed that emotions are actually the most important inspiring forces and are predictors of behaviors.

When it comes to emotions, organization is a primary characteristic. When anger is aroused in a person the probability increases that the person's activities will be directed and continued towards a particular direction or target. When friendliness and sympathy is aroused it is most likely that the person's behavior will be aimed at a certain direction. The more robust the emotional procedure that is aroused, the more certain the person's behavior will be managed in a way that is dependable on the emotional reaction.

One of the well-known theories of intelligence was introduced in the early 1920s and it proposed that there are two factors which lie beneath human intelligence: specific factors and a general factor. First, the specific factors are distinctive to a person's performance on cognitive tests, while the next, general factor transcends all intelligent tasks. Researchers have asserted that a person's general intelligence offers an indication of the person's level of intellectual activity and may be used as a means to predict success in school.

It has been argued about general intelligence that it is comprised of fluid and crystallized intelligences. Fluid intelligence is described as the ability to identify the relationships among the assorted concepts which are independent of experience and the ability of problem-solving. Fluid intelligence is how a person finds meaning from knowledge and not just the person's knowledge itself. On the other hand, crystallized intelligence is the capability to make use of knowledge, experience and skill that a person has been able to gain over time.

The ability of an individual to perceive, manage, express, understand and use one's emotions in a positive and enriching way can be broadly classified as emotional intelligence (EQ). If you want to achieve happiness and success in your personal and professional life, you will need to concentrate on developing your EQ rather than just your intellectual abilities.

There is a lot of evidence to prove that EQ will help you gain confidence, channelize your emotions in the most productive way possible and achieve your short-term and long-term goals and aspirations.

Emotional Intelligence can be broadly classified into four distinct areas. Self-awareness, self-management, social awareness and relationship management are the four core areas that will help you manage your emotions in the best possible way.

All human beings are controlled by emotions and individuals who manage them positively have been found to be very successful both in their personal and professional life. The brain can be broadly divided as emotional and intellectual. As we perceive intellect to be more important that emotions we tend to use that part of the brain that develops your intellectual abilities.

When you start engaging the emotional part of the brain you will be able to not just understand your own emotions but that of others too. This will help you connect well with others and you will become popular among family and friends.

How does emotional intelligence help connect to your emotions?

Emotions dominate our thinking process and all good and bad decisions are based on the emotions that we feel during decision making. When you are stressed you stop thinking in a rational way and lose the important connect with your emotional side. EQ will help you reestablish the connection between decision making and emotions by making you understand its meaning.

The emotions that we feel can be both positive and negative. Although it is not possible to completely eliminate negative feelings you will still be able to control and channelize them properly.

There are various emotional signals that we convey verbally and non-verbally. EQ will help you interpret these signals so that there is no miscommunication. The communications between the sender and the receiver will become positive when the chances of been misinterpreted are reduced and eliminated.

Self-awareness about the wide range of emotions that you feel will help build your self-confidence. You would be able to manage and utilize them in the best possible way.

EQ will help you perceive and understand the emotions of others. This will enhance your ability to think and react positively.

It is important to connect with your core emotions and be comfortable with them. This will help you know about your true feelings and you would be able to accomplish more. EQ will help you deal with challenges better as you will be able to control your emotions even during stressful situations.

You would be able to stay focused and not let emotions get the better of you. This would help in resolution of conflicts as you will be able to understand the view point of others. The skills of emotional intelligence will help you recognize your emotional state and that of others in an effective way and this can pave the way for success.

Emotional Intelligence in the Workplace

The foundation component to effective performance in a vast majority of jobs is emotional intelligence. It has been claimed that it is EQ rather than IQ which predicts top performance among employees. The stress on emotional intelligence as being foundational for effective job performance has increased. This is because as workers move up to management positions and have the skills or abilities to affect those workers that are dependent on them for leadership

Almost 90% of competencies required for success at work are made up of social and emotional focus when in leadership positions. Leaders need to communicate and cultivate a vision within the organizations that their workers are encouraged to support. A leader's cultivation of a vision in order to communicate to employees is an activity of both the head and the heart.

To put it simply, leading is not merely a cognitive or analytical competency which is complete in its own merit, but more accurately the cognitive competency is a threshold skill which must be complemented by the distinguishing competencies within the realm of emotional intelligence. Distinguishing competencies can become more critical as workers move into higher level leadership positions and can separate the star performers from the average performers in the organization.

The focus of emotionally intelligent leadership is on using the relationship and emotional know-how in order to encourage and motivate others into accomplishing workplace goals that tackle the needs of the employees, the organization and the customers. An intrinsic feature of emotional intelligence is self-awareness. A leader's self-awareness is important in order to be able to watch or monitor him or herself, observe him or herself in action, to affect his or her actions so that they work for his or her benefit.

In the regular interactions which leaders experience, it is obvious that leaders would be best aided if they were skilled in the EI areas of self-management and self-awareness. It has been discovered that people who have skills in the area of emotional intelligence competency of self-management contributed more than 70% more to the success of an organization than those who have weaker emotional intelligence in the area. The skill to successfully support workers and the organizational goals of the firm improved with effectual emotional intelligence skills showed that teams working for the leaders who have had training were able to grow their organizations at a higher rate than those who have leaders with less skill.

There are specific competencies that are used to predict the performance of a leader and they include: (1) intellectual or cognitive ability like systems thinking; (2)

intrapersonal abilities or self-management like adaptability; and, (3) interpersonal or relationship management like networking. The competencies of relationship management and self-management are made of emotional intelligence skills.

So as to support the improvement of leadership skills, as proposed within the relationship management and self-management competencies, the techniques of role playing, social reinforcement, modeling, and transfer of training. This is centered on training in new behavior which is based upon training which precedes attitude changes and understanding of the intellectual basis of new behavior.

Why Is Emotional Intelligence So Important To Ensure Success

If you want to be successful in life, emotional intelligence is a very important aspect that will help propel you towards it with ease. Although most people tend to give a lot of importance to IQ (intelligence quotient), you would be surprised to know that EQ (emotional quotient) is as important and in some cases more important than IQ.

Individuals who have high EQ tend to be more successful in their relationships (both professional and personal), will be able to effectively deal with others and succeed in their goals. Apart from this you would also be able to identify, control and manage your emotions positively. There is often a misconception that individuals with high EQ are emotional. However on the contrary such individuals are able to control their emotions better and this helps them perform better.

Most people who are brilliant academically and have very IQ tend to be less successful at the workplace. However some managers who might not possess very high IQ tends to be very successful professionally. Emotional intelligence skills give managers the edge that they need to achieve success both as individuals and as a team.

There are various characteristics of emotional intelligence that will help you understand other people's emotions and using this you would be able to deal with your boos, peers and sub-ordinates in the best possible way. These EQ characteristics include empathy, managing relationships, self-awareness, self-motivation and mood management.

How Can Emotional Intelligence Ensure Success

Improve both verbal and nonverbal communication skills and this will help you communicate with others in an open and honest way. As your communication skills improve you will be able to put forth your ideas and views in an effective manner.

Identify and share your feelings with others. Apart from this you would also be able to understand other people's views and opinions easily. When you acknowledge the other person's point of view and not try to impose your opinion on others, it will help build team spirit within the organization.

Individuals with high EQ will be able to come up with more solutions for any problem as they will be widening their horizon to include not just their opinion but that of others too. As you will not be stressed, it will help you think in a clear way and your decision making abilities will increase significantly.

It will also help in having realistic goals and take positive steps to achieve them in a systematic way. Most of the time our success at work is not just dependent on our individual abilities but also that of our team. When you learn how to interact with others at work, you would be able to motivate and encourage all members of your team to achieve their individual and organizational goals.

You will also be able to learn how to take responsibility for your actions. When you start caring about others at work, it will help you build a bond of trust among all team members. Most of us tend to be impulsive with our behavior and feelings and you can use emotional intelligence to help control such behavior. There are various triggers to the way we behave and when we are able to control them, you are most likely to achieve success at work.

A very important thing that you need to remember is that it takes time and effort to develop emotional intelligence. These skills cannot be learned overnight. However when you do make the effort to learn these skills, you will be able to reap the benefits of it all through your personal and professional life.

Why Emotional intelligence is Important?

There is often a misconception among people that the only skill needed to succeed in life is IQ (intelligence quotient) or intellectual skills. You would be surprised to know that a mere twenty percent of our success is dependent on intellectual skills. A whopping eighty percent of success both in your personal and professional life is dependent on emotional intelligence or emotional quotient (EQ).

You would be able to perceive and understand your emotions as well as those of others when you start using emotional intelligence skills. This is one of the key concepts that will help you achieve your goals. Your self-confidence will improve and this can help you perform better.

The Importance of Emotional Intelligence

All our decisions are based on emotions and you would be able to accurately identify your emotions and feelings when you start using EQ skills. It can be the most important differentiating factor between success and failure. When you know how you are feeling during a particular situation, you would be able to handle your emotions positively and this can create various opportunities for you.

When you are stressed you would not be able to think in a rational way and this can have a big impact on your decision making abilities. Emotional intelligence will help bring down your stress levels and you will be able to start thinking in a calm way once again.

We communicate verbally but most of our communication tends to happens in a non-verbal way. The communications skills will be improved and you would be able to understand the non-verbal cues that you receive from others.

You would be able to deal with challenges in an effective way when you start using emotional intelligence skills. When you start managing your emotions positively you would be able to look at things in a new perspective. This will help you understand the view point of others. Conflict resolution will become easier due to this.

For every problem that you face you would be able to come up with multiple solutions. Your thinking will not be limited and you would be able to think of unconventional solutions.

You would be able to connect with others easily as you will understand their point of view. This will help you develop and maintain good relationships with everyone. You would be able to work well in a team and this will increase your productivity.

You would be able to focus on your goals and achieve them easily as your mind will be free of negative thoughts. As you would not be stressed and be able to identify the triggers that cause them, you would be able to control them easily and stay healthy.

Most experts acknowledge the contribution of emotional intelligence in an individual's success story. Due to this it has gained a lot of popularity and more and more people have started using these skills. Nowadays there is a lot of significance attached to learning the skills of emotional intelligence for a successful life.

Dimensions of Emotional Intelligence

The ability of an individual to identify and control their emotions and that of others can be broadly termed as emotional intelligence (EI). Although most of us think that personal emotions should have no place in the decision making process, it is often quite difficult to separate emotions and decision making.

Individuals who are aware of their emotions will be able to understand the situations that make them feel the way they do. If you learn how to manage your feelings, you will be able to achieve a lot of personal and professional success. So instead of assuming that emotions are not important at the workplace, it would be best if you learn to use them in a productive manner.

There are various dimensions of emotional intelligence and it would be best if you are aware about them as they will help you manage your emotions better.

Self-awareness – Individuals who have high EI are aware about their feelings and emotions. Due to this awareness they are able to control and channelize their feelings much better. They will also know about their emotional strengths and weaknesses and this helps them in the process of decision making.

Self-regulation or handling emotions – Most people lack the ability to control their emotions and they act impulsively due to this. They let emotions get the better of them and this can cause a lot of problems. You would be able to control your impulses through self-regulation and this will help you stay positive and calm even in stressful situations.

Motivation – You would be able to set goals and work towards achieving them when you are motivated. People with EI generally have high levels of motivation than others. Perseverance and persistence in spite of the odds been stacked against them are characteristics of people who are motivated. This helps increase their productivity and they would be able to achieve big and small goals effectively.

Empathy – The ability to understand the other person's point of view can be broadly classified as empathy. When you are able to recognize the feelings of others, it will help you look at things in a new perspective. It will also help in conflict resolution and you would be able to work better as a team. People with empathy are good listeners and this helps them manage others easily.

Social Skills – People with high EI have the ability to get along well with others. They would be able to work better in a team due to their ability to make friends. As they are helpful towards others they would be able to build strong relationships that are long lasting and fruitful. Apart from this they would also be able to manage conflicts and lead their team towards success. Confidence and communications skills will also be high when you have good social skills.

Emotional intelligence is the skill that you will need to learn and develop if you want to become successful in life. The five dimensions of EI are crucial for its development.

Self-management defined

Emotions dictate the way we react in everyday life and self-management will help us manage them in an effective way even in stressful situations. You would be able to build your emotional intelligence (EI) when you learn how to manage your thoughts and reactions. We can choose the way we respond to any situation when you learn self-management or self-regulation.

By controlling your emotions you would be able to choose how you will react to situations and people. Self-management will also make you feel positive as you will be able to adapt to changing circumstances easily. You would be able to control your impulsive thoughts and behavior by successfully self-regulating your emotions.

When you start paying close attention about how you think and feel you would be able to self-manage your behavior. You would need to take the initiative and this will help you control your feelings in an effective manner.

7 simple things you need to know about self-management

1. It is important that you are aware about your emotions as you will be able to choose the way you react to people and different situations that you face in everyday life. This will help you adapt well even in difficult situations.

2. Self-regulation will help keep negative reactions under control. There are many negative emotions that human beings experience daily. These can be anger, fear, violence and frustration. When you feel such emotions you will not be able to think in a clear way and this can affect your decision making capabilities.

3. There are various situations when negative feelings or emotions can be triggered and knowledge about such situations will help you manage them in a positive way.

4. As your thoughts and moods not just affect you but also those around you, it is important to self-manage them. So instead of thinking impulsively you will need to take time to think about the situation and take a decision in a calm way.

5. When you are stressed, you would not be able to manage your emotions and this can make it very difficult to motivate yourself towards success. You will be able to manage stress effectively when you self-regulate your emotional process.

6. Identifying emotions that are negative will help you replace them with positive thoughts. You will need to think of ways to do this. You would be able to achieve this only through regular practice.

7. If you are faced with a difficult situation, it would be best if you avoid taking any decisions. Taking time out to self-manage your emotions will help you choose the best solution to any problem.

When you start regulating emotions you will be able to respond in an appropriate way. Decision making will not be done in haste and this will help save you a lot of trouble. Apart from this, you will also be able to respond better to others thoughts and feelings.

Controlling and evaluating emotions will help you improve your emotional intelligence skills.

Relationship Management

Relationship management is an essential emotional intelligence (EI) skill that will help you connect with others. You would be able to develop and maintain good relationship with others by using this skill. It will help you manage conflict and you would be able to work better in a team.

There are four components of EI including self-awareness, self-management, social awareness and relationship management. Individuals who are good at the first three components have been found to be effective in relationship management and this makes them very good leaders.

It is often very difficult to predict how people will react in a particular situation. When you work together in a team it is important that you understand each other's view point. This will help build team spirit and increase productivity.

You would be able to manage the way people respond in any situation by motivating them. When you become aware of your own emotions, you would be able to recognize the thoughts and feelings of others in an effective way.

What are the 5 important things you need to know about relationship management?

It is advisable to recognize the need for change and make some effort to support this process. You will need to communicate the need for change to all members of the team in an effective way. Failure to do so will see resistance to change as they will start seeing it as something that is been forced on them.

When you become aware of your emotions, you would be able to manage them better and these skills will help you manage your relationships easily. You would be able to build competencies and develop new strengths.

Provide a vision that helps motivate others. You would be able to persuade people by providing feedback and building skills. This will help in instilling positive feelings. They would also become aware of their strengths and weaknesses and use this in a productive way.

Communication is vital in relationship management and when you interact with others you will be able to achieve the desired results. It is important to remember that communication is not just verbal skills but also nonverbal cues that help you understand what the other person is trying to convey.

Inspire and motivate team members by knowing about their strengths and desires. This will help you channelize and align their desires with that of the organization or business.

You will need to focus on building relationship over a period of time. This process does not happen overnight and you will need to put a lot of effort. This will help in building trust among team members.

Relationship management will help you put things into perspective. You would be able to overcome problems and setbacks by inspiring creative problem solving among your team members. The quality of your relationship will determine how well you connect with others. You will be able to find new opportunities when you make this skill an integral part of your everyday life.

Measuring Emotional Intelligence

Emotions affect the way we take decisions in life and more and more people now accept that emotional intelligence (EI) is very important for personal and professional success than the conventional intelligence. The number of organizations who are hiring candidates on the basis of EI has been on the increase as they have started realizing the importance of this skill at the workplace.

Emotions not just affect us but also people around us. You would be able to relate well with others when you have high EI and this will help you succeed in all aspects of life. When you start understanding and valuing other people's thoughts and feelings, you would be able to resolve conflicts and this will help in the decision making process.

Emotional intelligence will help you take responsibility for your actions. You will be able to analyze each decision of yours in a rational manner without emotions getting the better of you. It will also help you work better in a team.

People have different personalities and have developed unique ways of showing and interpreting emotions. If you are able to understand and interpret your emotions and those of people around you, it will help you become more successful in life.

Emotional intelligence can be measured and it will help you understand how to manage emotions in an effective way. There are various tools that are widely used to measure EI and taking these tests will help in determining what your emotional quotient is.

Here is a list of some of the most popular tools that are used to measure EI:

MSCEIT Emotional Intelligence test – There are four skills of EI that are measured in this test. These skills include how to accurately perceive emotions, how to facilitate thought using emotions, understanding your emotions and those of others and managing emotions.

Multifactor Emotional Intelligence Scale – The ability of an individual to identify, perceive, understand and manage emotions is tested through a series of tasks.

EIQ – In this test the individual is assessed by his colleagues and managers using 360 questionnaires. This will be an all-round assessment of the individuals at their workplace.

ECI (Emotional competence inventory) – There are various competencies that are linked to EI and using these individuals will be assessed by people who know them.

Six Seconds Emotional Intelligence test – The test is based on various factors like adaptability, accountability, alignment, collaboration, leadership and trust.

All these assessment tools can be used to test and improve your emotional intelligence. The test results would be different depending on the age and gender of the individual whose EI is been measured. These tools are useful in not just knowing about your emotional state but also those of others. However there is some controversy on whether EI can be measured in an effective way.

When emotional intelligence is measured, you will be able to do a self-evaluation of all your strengths and weaknesses. This will help in developing and improving your skills. The various skills necessary for developing EI can be learned and the various assessment tools can be helpful in this regard.

What is Self-Awareness?

Self-awareness is one of the central ideas of emotional intelligence (EI). It is your ability to recognize your own emotions. When you start becoming aware of your innermost thoughts and feelings, you would be able to identify your emotional strengths and weaknesses.

Our moods and emotions not just affect us and our decision making process but also those around us. When you start understanding why you feel in a certain way, you would be able to control your thought process and not let it get affected by negative emotions.

Emotional intelligence has become increasingly important at the workplace and most employers have started hiring employees based on this skill. You would be surprised to know that most people are not aware of their emotions and this can affect their personal and professional growth. With coaching and training EI can be developed and you will become aware of your and other people's feelings and thoughts.

Why is Self-Awareness so important?

Self-awareness will help you see how an emotion is influencing your thought process. This will help you control the state of your mind and you can start using this to improve your decision making skills.

When you become self-aware, you would be able to step back and look at each thought and feeling that your mind processes in a rational way. This will also help you see how your decisions can affect others.

 You will start introspecting about who you really are, why you do things in a particular way, you would be able to increase your level of self-awareness. This will help you come up with so many alternatives that you thought were not possible.

Awareness of your emotions will help you control them and they would not be able to able to get the upper hand. You would be able to choose your reaction to any situation and not be dictated by emotions. This means that you can also turn your negative thoughts to positive.

We experience different kinds of emotions (positive and negative) each day. When you start understanding the emotions that you experience, you will start recognizing the strengths that need to be developed and weaknesses that need to be controlled and eliminated. This will help develop your self-confidence.

You would be able to focus on things that are important. The number of possibilities that will be open to you will also increase. When you have more options available to you, it will help choose the best alternative.

Initially it will take some time to become aware of your innermost emotions. When you start spending time to build self-awareness, you would be able to increase your EI. You will not become overwhelmed with emotions as you will be taking the first step of developing emotional intelligence. You will be able to delve into a deeper emotional level and start practicing self-awareness in your everyday life. This will help you communicate clearly and achieve all your goals and aspirations.

What is Social Awareness?

Social awareness is a very important component of emotional intelligence (EI). It helps in understanding how you need to become aware of what others think about you. This is also known as empathy and is often considered one of the most important skills necessary for success both in your personal and professional life.

When you start understanding the emotions and needs of other people, you would be able to improve your EI easily. If you do not give importance to other people's thoughts and feelings, you will be considered insensitive and uncaring.

It is quite surprising to know that the ability to understand other people feelings is lacking in most people. As most of our decisions not just affect us but other too, it would be advisable it you also take their view point into consideration. This will help you take decisions that are beneficial for everyone.

6 simple steps to build social awareness

Most people are not self-aware because they do not bother to listen to others. They are often seen giving more importance to their thought process than others. If you want to improve your emotional intelligence, you will need to start listening to others. Improving communication skills will be crucial for developing this skill.

When you interact with other people, you will need to pay close attention to what they are saying and why they are saying it in a particular way. This will help you understand the concerns of other people.

When you listen attentively to what the other person is saying, you will be able to ask questions about things that will affect you.

Body language, face expressions and tone of voice are things that you will need to notice when talking with others. There are various emotional cues that are hidden in these gestures and this will help you take better decisions.

When you show empathy, it does not necessary that you accept the other person's point of view. By giving importance to their thoughts and ideas, you are acknowledging the fact that they their view point should also be heard before the process of decision making takes effect.

You would also need to pay attention to your feelings as the view point of the other person can affect your emotional state of mind. Self-awareness will you become socially aware.

Your ability to respond to change will also improve significantly when you become aware of what around you are thinking.

When you recognize the feelings and thoughts of others, you are not just been considerate but also becoming socially aware. You would be able to build a long lasting relationship with the individual whose view point you take into consideration. It will also help gain their trust.

New opportunities will be created when you become socially aware. Your self-confidence will improve and you will start feeling socially comfortable. This will also enable you to work better in a team. Social awareness is a crucial aspect of emotional intelligence and this skill helps individuals blossom into leaders.

How to Improve Emotional Intelligence

Although you are supposed to suppress emotions at the workplace, you would be surprised to know that emotions, moods and feelings play a major role in determining your success in the organization. Interaction among different members of a team will determine whether targets are achieved, conflicts are resolved and better relationships are built and all these factors are based on the emotions you feel at the workplace.

Human beings will not be able to separate emotions when they take professional decisions. Emotions affect every aspect of their interaction and decision making abilities. Individuals who are able to control their emotions positively have been found to be more successful at the workplace.

When you are able to recognize and understand your emotions, you will be able to increase your productivity and help others to perform better. Businesses that allow their employees to express their emotions openly have been found to benefit from it. They would be able to build team spirit and achieve all their goals and objectives. It will also help in conflict resolution.

When individuals are not allowed to express their emotions at the workplace it will only help build bitterness and conflict. It can also have a negative influence on the overall on the overall work performed by the team. Stress will increase and productivity will go down.

Emotional intelligence skills are not just important for managers and leaders. All employees who work in an organization should be trained to acquire these skills so that they can contribute to the betterment of the organization.

Managers who will be able to manage their emotions and that of others will be able to motivate and build loyalty among all team members. They would also be able to understand the emotional needs of others and this will greatly help in conflict resolution at the workplace.

How to improve emotional intelligence at the workplace?

Self-awareness about your emotions will help you understand the significance of what you are feeling. Due to this you would be able to control how you react in a particular situation. When you learn to recognize and manage your emotions at the workplace you will be able to achieve the desired results easily.

Empathy is putting you in other people's shoes and trying to look at things from their perspective. When you are able to understand the other person's point of view you will be able to resolve conflicts and build strong bonds among different members of the team.

Learn to share your emotions with others in a positive way. This will also encourage others to share their emotions with you. When you start sharing emotion this way, you will be able to come up with many options for every situation. When you allow people to express their anger and frustration, you will be giving them an opportunity to get rid of

It is advisable to have realistic goals that can be achieved. Emotional intelligence will also help you look at things in an optimistic way. When you start listening to other people you will be able to broaden your horizon and avoid any misunderstanding.

All individuals want to be heard and be given an opportunity to express themselves. When this opportunity is provided by their managers or leaders it helps resolve conflicts. Apart from this it will also help in reducing stress. This will help them think clearly as stress can cloud their thinking abilities.

Businesses that help build emotional intelligence across all levels of employees will be able to maintain a positive environment in the organization. This will help increase productivity and build team spirit within the organization.

How to Improve Emotional Intelligence Skills

The emotional intelligence of each individual is different as it is dependent on so many factors. EQ (emotional quotient) usually refers to a person's ability to control their emotions in a positive way and this can greatly impact their success in all aspects of life.

You will come across various kinds of people at the workplace. People with high EQ will be less stressful, happier and also popular among colleagues and friends. It is not they are extremely intelligent but they do have the ability to control their emotions and recognize the emotions of others too around them easily.

When you start learning and using the skills of emotional intelligence you will not only be able to identify and control your emotions but also those of others around you. EQ is a skill that can be learned easily and you not require any special characteristics to become proficient in it.

There are many individuals who are able to identify their emotional state but are unable to express it properly. This could make them get angry with themselves and others. When you are able to identify and utilize your emotions, you would be able to improve your ability to deal with others in an effective manner.

5 Steps to Improve Emotional Intelligence Skills

If you are keen on developing your emotional intelligence skills, you will first need to observe how you behave and react in different situations. You will be able to learn a lot when you start making this observation. It is equally important to observe and study the behavior of others towards specific situations.

You will need to evaluate all your strength and weaknesses. This will help you work on areas where you are weak. You would be able to improve your EQ skills when you start focusing on things that need your immediate attention.

Most people shy away from taking responsibility for their actions. However when you do start taking responsibility for your actions you will become better at managing relationships and taking decisions wisely.

Empathy is one of the most important emotional intelligence skills that you need to develop to become successful in life. When you are able to identify what the other person wants, feel and desire you will be able to take decisions by recognizing the feelings of others. You will also stop judging others based on any pre-conceived notions when you start building empathy.

Although it is not possible to avoid stress there are ways to manage it positively. When you develop emotional intelligence you will be able to handle stressful situations easily as you are in better control of your emotions. You will be able to stay calm even in stressful situations and this will help improve your decision making ability.

As you become more aware of how your actions will affect others, you will start paying attention to how you behave and react in various day to day situations. Your personal and professional success is dependent to a large extent on how quickly you are able to learn and adapt the various emotional intelligence skills to your life. You will also be able to reduce stress as you would have identified the factors that help trigger it

You will need to make an honest attempt to learn the various emotional intelligence skills necessary to become successful in life. Analyze how every action of yours will affect others and based on this analysis you will need to start taking decisions that take other people's emotions too in mind. You will be able to improve your self-confidence and interpersonal skills too through emotional intelligence.

Emotional Intelligence & Conflict Resolution

Conflicts are an inevitable part of life – whether personal or professional life. They involve both feelings and facts. Facts are usually easier to get and are very helpful as the point to start with. However, facts do not make up the only part of the entire story. There is a need to go beyond the facts in order to understand the reason why the facts are important to the people involved. There is a need to find and understand the feelings that underlie the conflict and the needs and wants (unstated) of the people involved in the conflict.

It becomes crucial to try and probe into what the people in conflict are feeling. They need to be listened to empathically and focus must be given to the language conveyed by both their words and body language. There are times when questions need to be asked regarding how they feel. People in conflicts will generally feel angry, scared, threatened, sad, or even a combination of all of them (and then some). People can easily feel anger towards a remark of two by a colleague. Also, they may feel rather sad that their feelings have been hurt.

More often than not, someone involved in a conflict would be so open about discussing their feelings regarding the issues. Generally, people will remain unaware of the mix of emotions that they are actually feeling. This is an area where a supervisor or a manager can take charge of the situation and coax the people in conflict to reveal their true feelings, analyze them, and find ways to resolve the conflict.

The initial step is understanding feeling and then identifying the unstated need or want. There are some very common wants and they may be among the following:

Recognition

Importance

Promotions

Productivity

Being part of the community or group

More money

Self-expression

Love

When the underlying needs and wants of the people in conflict are understood, then the motivations of these people become clear. Only then can the leader and the parties involved work together to solve the problems that is the result of the underlying need or want.

When in conflict, there is a need to orient the self. Questions about what the real underlying feelings need to be found and understood. Then it is important to find out why those feelings have come to the fore and how the conflict can move the person further or nearer the need or want. Only after such tasks can the feelings of the other person be evaluated. Only then can one put one's self into the shoes of the other person. Once this has happened, we can then find ways to resolve the conflict.

The bottom line is, conflicts are an inevitable part of life and people need to be prepared for them and even expect them. The way the conflicts will be managed defines the leader. Once a leader remains calm and unbiased, exploring the emotions and the underlying wants and needs of the people involved, and finding ways to lead the parties to arrive at a resolution will strengthen the leader's relationship with the people involved.

Leading with Emotional Intelligence

The common factor that all leaders share and which helps them become successful in life is emotional intelligence (EI). This is the most important distinguishing skill that will help you achieve success both in your personal and professional life. Businesses big and small have realized the importance of EI and have started placing emphasis on hiring people who have this skill.

Nowadays most people are stressed and this can prevent them from thinking rationally. This also affects their decision making capabilities. If you want to be successful at the workplace you will need to understand and manage your emotions and those of others around you. Every aspect of your day to day life gets affected by emotional intelligence.

7 steps to leading with emotional intelligence

You will need to understand the importance of self-awareness and self-management. This will help you manage emotions in a productive and constructive way.

Most people tend to be disconnected with their emotional state of mind. Due to this they would be unable to communicate their thoughts and feelings in an effective way. When you start paying attention to your emotions, it will help improve decision making.

Self-awareness will help you understand how emotions affect all aspects of our life. They influence your behavior, decision making, feelings and thoughts. You will be able to assess your competencies and this will help increase your EI levels. This will also help manage change in an effective way.

Areas for improvement need to be identified and this can be done by understanding the impact that emotions have at your workplace. This will also help improve work relationship.

Learning how to manage emotions in stressful situations will help improve personal performance. You will also be able to manage conflicts in a positive way.

Empathy is critical for understanding the thoughts and feelings of others in your team. It is important to understand the view point of other people and this will help build team spirit.

Good communication is not just verbal skills; you need to be aware of the nonverbal cues as well. It would be advisable to interpret facial expressions and body language of others to help improve your emotional intelligence.

When you develop the skills of EI, you would be able to meet all challenges in a positive way. You will also start looking at things in a new perspective and this will help you come up with many alternatives.

You will not be able to master the skills of EI just by reading about them; you would actually need to connect with the emotional side of your personality in such a way that it helps produce the necessary change in you.

Emotional intelligence skills can be learned by anyone by practicing them in your everyday life. It will take patience and perseverance to learn these skills. Although you need to put in a bit of effort to learn the skills, the rewards would definitely make it worthwhile.

Project Management, Leadership, and Emotional Intelligence

There have been studies have revealed that managers with competency leadership styles and emotional intelligence have influenced, positively, their organization's performance, and using several leadership styles is apt for different organizational perspectives.

According to the emotional intelligence model by Daniel Goleman, there are 19 leadership competencies that have been identified and grouped into four dimensions which are relationship management, social awareness, self-awareness and self-management. There have also been 6 different organizational situations that have been introduced with the proper leadership style and accompanying competencies and profiles for every situation. Leadership styles are (1) commanding, (2) pacesetting, (3) affiliative, (4) democratic, (5) coaching and (6) visionary. Among these, the last four are the leadership styles which are considered as sufficient for most of the situations from mid-term to long-term organizational objectives. The first two styles tend to work rather well for recovery situations.

According to the school of thought for competency leadership, there are fifteen leadership competencies which are grouped and make three types of competency: emotional competency, managerial competency, and intellectual competency. There are 3 leadership styles which are (1) engaging, (2) involving, and (3) goal oriented. As per the three styles, goal oriented leaders are those that prove to be best when it comes to handling projects of low complexity, involved leaders are at their best when it comes to handling projects of medium complexity, and those who are engaged leaders are at their best handling high-complexity projects.

Studies that explored the relationship between the three competence types (emotional, managerial and intellectual) and the success of a project found that the significant contributor to project success is emotional competence. Managerial competence, on the other hand, only contributes occasionally to the success of a project. It has also been found that intellectual competence, on certain occasions, correlated negatively.

Leaders and managers who are emotionally intelligent tend to create more positive work environments, work more effectively, create better cooperation and more trust among workers through interpersonal relations, and express more commitment to the organization they work for. Though there are many general management skills included in project management controlling, allocating resources, planning, leadership skills are needed in order to manage the human resource elements of projects successfully.

A project is defined as an endeavor, temporary in nature, which is undertaken in order to create a result, product, or service which then creates 3 difficult conditions for project leadership. Primary and the most important, temporary projects don't continue long-term leadership development and improvement. Second, the organization of projects outlines a range of structures from project-ized to functional, based on the structure of the performing organizations with numerous matrix formats in between. The project manager has anywhere between total authority and no authority, in such organizational settings, over the members of the project team based on the project's organizational structure.

Nevertheless, the ultimate responsibility of the outcome of the projects rests solely with the project manager. Therefore, the possession of strong leadership abilities is highly critical for project success. Projects oftentimes are initiated with team members who do not know each other and this requires the project managers to have emotional competencies like relationship management, self-management, self-awareness and social awareness.

Why All Employees Need Emotional Intelligence Training

Emotional intelligence is a skill which enables an individual to examine what and why he or she feels a certain way in a particular situation. Being able to develop a high level of emotional intelligence benefits people in any field and being able to examine thoughts and emotions closely before making decisions or giving verbal responses lead to more success both at work and at home. This makes it very important for employees to receive emotional intelligence training.

Emotional Intelligence -- Characteristics

There are five elements which define EI, and they are:

Self-awareness – Employees who have high EI are usually self-aware. They are able to understand their emotions which make them able to avoid letting their feelings rule their actions. They are usually confident as they do not allow their emotions to go out of control and they trust their intuition.

Motivation – Employees who have high emotional intelligence are generally motivated. These are people who are able to take a long-term view of things. They are able to defer any immediate results for long-term success. Motivated people are very productive and enjoy being challenged. They generally enjoy their work and are highly efficient and effective.

Self-regulation – Workers who have the ability to control their impulses and emotions are highly sought after. This is because they normally will not allow themselves to succumb to feelings of jealousy or anger. They do not make decisions carelessly or impulsively. These are employees who think before they act. Self-regulated individuals are able to ensure that they analyze a situation first before they react to it.

Empathy – Empathy is one of the most crucial elements of EI. It is the ability to understand and identify what other people's views are, their wants, and their needs. People who have a high degree of empathy are able to "walk in the other person's shoes." They are very good are recognizing the feelings of other people though such feelings may not be made obvious. This makes such people excellent relationship managers. They are great listeners and are very good in relating with others. Such people do not stereotype and judge others quickly.

Social Skills – People who have very good social skills are generally easy to get along with and speak to. Having good social skills is a sigh of having high emotional intelligence. Such people are very good at being team players. They tend to be very good at helping other people shine and develop. Employees with good social skills are very good communicators and can build and manage relationships very easily.

Emotional intelligence is a key to success and developing high EI is always beneficial to a person in all facets of his or her life. As the ability to manage relationships and people is crucial for leaders and managers, emotional intelligence training is important to ensure that they develop the necessary skills to be successful in their work.

High emotional intelligence means a person is able to get along with co-workers; is productive, can control emotions, empathize with others and communicate well, among others. Such skills are highly prized within organizations.

What functions Do Emotions Serve

Organizations are measured by its value in terms of stocks or profits. When it comes to members of the workforce, the value of their job is emotional as well. The word "emotion" is derived from a French term which means "to stir up." A more formal definition would be that it is an intense, short feeling that results from an event. People do not react to a situation the same way. For example, a supervisor's manner of speaking may be perceived by one employee as pleasant and motivating, while another employee may take it as threatening. Emotions may influence whether an individual is receptive to getting advice, how they perform as an individual or as part of a team, and whether they will stay or quit. Emotions can either be positive or be negative. This is where *emotional intelligence (EQ)* plays a role.

Emotions help to shape a person's belief about the value of a team, a company, or a job. They can also affect a person's behavior at work. According to research, it has been found that the people within one's inner circle are much better able to understand and recognize one's emotions. One method of managing the effects of so called "emotional labor" is through increasing one's awareness of the disparities between the real emotions being felt and the emotions that are required in the job or professional persona. Questions like "what am I feeling and what are the feelings of others around me?" form the core of *emotional intelligence (EQ)*.

The term *emotional intelligence (EQ)* was originally thought up by two psychologists named Peter Salovey and by John Mayer. It was then made much more popular by another psychologist, this time a man by the name of Daniel Goleman. *Emotional intelligence (EQ)* looks at by what means individuals can understand others better through the development of increased awareness of the emotions they feel and that of others.

When it comes to developing a high or increased level of *emotional intelligence (EQ)*, there are building blocks – four of them. Self-awareness occurs when one is able to precisely observe, evaluate, and also exhibit the appropriate emotion. Self-management happens when one is effectively able to guide one's emotions, when needed, in a positive manner. Social awareness is present when one is able to understand the way others feel. Relationship management occurs when one is able to help other people to manage their emotions and sincerely build relationships that are supportive.

At work, *emotional intelligence (EQ)* can be employed to build harmonious groups or teams by making use of the talents of each group or team member. For this to happen, people who are knowledgeable about *emotional intelligence (EQ)* can watch out for opportunities to inspire other people to work while also motivating themselves. Foremost among the emotions that help to create successful groups or teams is empathy which is the ability to "wear the other person's shoe," regardless of whether that person has managed to achieve a major goal or has fallen short.

Employees who have high *emotional intelligence (EQ)* have been discovered to have advanced self-efficacy in coping with difficulties, observe situations as challenges instead of threats, and possess better life satisfaction that helps to lower levels of stress.

Emotional Intelligence and Leadership Styles

You will find that individuals with high emotional intelligence are successful in their chosen career and are natural leaders. Success in leadership is usually attributed to high levels of EQ (emotional quotient) and not IQ (intelligence quotient). Without these skills leaders will not be effective in their jobs. There are individuals who have all the necessary leadership qualities but lack in emotional intelligence skills. Such individuals will not be able to become effective leaders.

Individuals with emotional intelligence skills will be able to manage multiple roles and meet all the challenges in their organization easily. Leaders are usually responsible for maintaining a positive emotional atmosphere both within and outside the organization. This will help reduce stress and you will be able to take decisions that are in the interest of everyone in the organization.

Although all leaders plan their task in advance, it is not necessary that things go as planned. Leaders will need to manage their emotions during such bad days and stay focused. Emotional intelligence will give leaders the necessary skills to achieve their goals.

What are the leadership styles of emotional intelligence?

The best leadership style that you can adopt is democratic where you will listen to the opinion of others before taking a decision. You will work together as a team and this will enable you to come up with more solutions for day to day problems. Everyone in the team will be able to participate and this will create trust and understating between all team members.

The next leader ship style would be visionary where they show enormous foresight on the future plans of the organization. In this leadership style there will be many long term and short term goals set for the organization.

Delegation of responsibility is common among leaders who adopt a delegate style of leadership. They will help individuals take responsibility for their actions and result in better outcomes. As leaders are aware of their strength and weaknesses they would be able to set realistic goals for their teams that can be achieved. Achievements will help build self-confidence and enable the team to fulfill all its goals.

Most managers use different types of leadership styles depending on the specific requirements of the project. This will also help them see situations from the other person's perspective and avoid unnecessary conflict. Irrespective of the situation they would be able to think in a rational way and not let emotions cloud their thinking capacity.

Although emotional intelligence skills help you manage your emotions better, it is sometimes difficult to express emotions that you do not feel. Your job performance and satisfaction are greatly dependent on how you are able to manage your emotions at work.

Businesses all over the world have started recognizing the importance of emotional intelligence and holding training programs to develop leadership candidates. These training programs will help develop leadership effectiveness of individuals who are groomed as potential leaders in an organization.

Good leaders understand the importance of maintaining a two way communication channel with their team so that every member of the team is able to understand the importance of the project. This will also help leaders get effective feedback from their team members on issues that affect work performance. When team members are encouraged to express their opinion without fear they would be able to provide valuable input to the work they are performing.

Leaders have always played an important role in the growth of the organization. The various leadership styles that they adopt will help them be empathetic towards others. Effective leaders will be able to use emotional intelligence to manage their emotions to help achieve their goals.

How Gender Affects Emotional Intelligence

Emotional intelligence will play a significant role in determining your career success irrespective of your gender. Previously only IQ (intelligence quotient) was considered necessary for success in any field. However only high IQ will not guarantee you success in your chosen career and you will need to have emotional intelligence skills to really become successful in your professional and personal life.

Emotional intelligence is the ability of an individual to understand their feelings and emotions and that of others too. When you are in control of your emotions, you would be able to avoid conflicts and improve your decision making. You will be able to have a competitive edge when you develop EQ skills.

Regardless of the gender moods, feelings and emotions play a very important role in determining how successful you are in an organization. Women are perceived to have greater emotional intelligence when compared to men. It is usually believed that women are more expressive in their emotions and better at interpersonal skills. Although most men are capable of recognizing their innermost emotions they lack the ability to express them openly.

The verbal skills of women are much more developed than men and they are more skilled at expressing their feelings. This tends to give them the edge in understanding other people's thoughts and emotions. Men usually tend to avoid expressing their emotions naturally and they would need to make an effort to do so.

Men and women also have different styles of communicating with other people. While women are better at reading nonverbal cues men seem to be adept at problem solving. Men are better at concealing their real emotions and displaying only those that are suitable for any given situation.

While both men and women may be good at certain aspects of emotional intelligence they would need to develop other traits that will help them become successful at the workplace.

What are the qualities that men and women need to develop emotional intelligence?

Awareness about the innermost emotions will help both men and women utilize it in the best possible way. It will allow individuals to interact better with others in the organization.

Manage emotions in a way that is constructive and productive for the team and organization as a whole. It will help them build strong relationships throughout their life. When they are able to manage and connect with their emotions and that of others they will be able to reduce stress and improve emotional intelligence.

Nonverbal communication skills are as important as verbal communication. You would be surprised to know that most individuals communicate through nonverbal cues and these need to be interpreted correctly to develop EQ.

Although conflict cannot be avoided there are various ways through which you would be able to resolve them in a positive way. Good interpersonal skills will help you resolve conflicts easily.

Individuals who have developed emotional intelligence skills are self-confident in their abilities. This will help them take responsibility for their decisions and mistakes. The workplace environment will also become more productive as positive relationships will develop within the organization.

Businesses are now hiring men and women who have high EQ skills as they are better at managing relationships. They will not just be able to motivate themselves but will be able to motivate others too. Apart from this they would be able to recognize and interpret other people's emotions easily.

Research has established a strong relationship between emotional intelligence and success at the workplace. Irrespective of gender, it has been found that people with high EQ skills are better equipped to become future leaders in an organization.

Communication and Project Outcome

It has been argued that project managers in top companies use a vast portion of their time communicating with their team members. It has also been noted that effective communication is very important in every facet of organizational behavior. Communication is considered as the most important skill in whatever discipline.

When studies were done to investigate communication within the members of the project team, the significance of successful communication between external and internal objects was explored. It was concluded that one of the key factors in most failed projects is effective communication.

It has been observed that the absence of efficient communication results into big hurdles in the project management and affects the project's outcome negatively. Communication that is well-controlled and well-understood indicates maturity. Immaturity of approaches in human communication compromises the project outcome's effectiveness.

It has been found that there are 17 key risk factors which contribute to project failure. Among them are (1) lack of communication with the user, (2) misunderstanding the requirements of the user, (3) lack of proper harmonization among different teams, (4) failure to convey improvements and modifications of project objectives and scope clearly, (5) misunderstanding the scope and the objectives of a project, (6) inappropriate allocation of roles and tasks, and (7) lack of satisfactory project handling skills in collaboration and coordination. These are risk factors that are clearly associated with the interpersonal and communication capabilities of project members.

There have been six factors that are identified as the root causes of the failures of information technology project: (1) project handling factors, (2) top management factors, (3) technological factors, (4) institutional factors, (5) complexity factors, (6) and process factors. In all the six failure factors, communication is the common theme. The interpersonal capability and communication skills of project managers are extremely critical in creating successful and mutual interaction, communication, and coordination with the various members of the project team and the other stakeholder.

Also noted is that any prior unresolved conflicts of project team members can influence their interactions and communications with other colleagues in the institution. There are barriers to communication that exist between the members of the project team, especially in the early days of the formation of the project, because they continue to carry on their experiences from the prior work environments as they interact within the current or present relationship setting.

The interpersonal skills of the project manager can create a work environment within which the members of the project team feel comfortable and trust each other to freely communicate. System failures can be classifies into four types and they are expectation, process, correspondence and interaction. There are five factors responsible for the process, expectation, and interaction failures and they are:

Ineffective communication among the members of the project teams (process, expectation, and interaction)

Inadequate accurate, complete, and appropriate and documentation (interaction and expectation)

Inappropriate or incomplete knowledge and shared understanding (interaction and expectation)

Poor and ineffective management (process)

Inadequate effective and systemic process (process)

Miscommunication is recognized as among the major factors in most project failures, especially when it comes to technology projects.

Emotional Intelligence & Conflict Resolution

Conflicts are an inevitable part of life – whether personal or professional life. They involve both feelings and facts. Facts are usually easier to get and are very helpful as the point to start with. However, facts do not make up the only part of the entire story. There is a need to go beyond the facts in order to understand the reason why the facts are important to the people involved. There is a need to find and understand the feelings that underlie the conflict and the needs and wants (unstated) of the people involved in the conflict.

It becomes crucial to try and probe into what the people in conflict are feeling. They need to be listened to empathically and focus must be given to the language conveyed by both their words and body language. There are times when questions need to be asked regarding how they feel. People in conflicts will generally feel angry, scared, threatened, sad, or even a combination of all of them (and then some). People can easily feel anger towards a remark of two by a colleague. Also, they may feel rather sad that their feelings have been hurt.

More often than not, someone involved in a conflict would be so open about discussing their feelings regarding the issues. Generally, people will remain unaware of the mix of emotions that they are actually feeling. This is an area where a supervisor or a manager can take charge of the situation and coax the people in conflict to reveal their true feelings, analyze them, and find ways to resolve the conflict.

The initial step is understanding feeling and then identifying the unstated need or want. There are some very common wants and they may be among the following:

Recognition

Importance

Promotions

Productivity

Being part of the community or group

More money

Self-expression

Love

When the underlying needs and wants of the people in conflict are understood, then the motivations of these people become clear. Only then can the leader and the parties involved work together to solve the problems that is the result of the underlying need or want.

When in conflict, there is a need to orient the self. Questions about what the real underlying feelings need to be found and understood. Then it is important to find out why those feelings have come to the fore and how the conflict can move the person further or nearer the need or want. Only after such tasks can the feelings of the other person be evaluated. Only then can one put one's self into the shoes of the other person. Once this has happened, we can then find ways to resolve the conflict.

The bottom line is, conflicts are an inevitable part of life and people need to be prepared for them and even expect them. The way the conflicts will be managed defines the leader. Once a leader remains calm and unbiased, exploring the emotions and the underlying wants and needs of the people involved, and finding ways to lead the parties to arrive at a resolution will strengthen the leader's relationship with the people involved.

The Impact of Stress on Workplace Aggression

Psychologists are aware with the fact that stress can cause aggression at the workplace. Even few decades ago, in the 1980s, many psychologists considered stress as an epidemic that was of universal scope. There have been many studies which have proved that frequent exposure to situations that are stressful can lead to increases in impulsive and maladaptive behaviors that can include aggressiveness.

There are also some studies that have proved that stress tends to affect women and men in different ways, although both show tend to, when confronted with stressful situations, show aggression in their own way. For that reason, exploring tolerance for stress in the office and its effect on aggression in the workplace may prove to be valuable to the study of workplace aggression.

There has been a survey done recently among UK workers that revealed stress being brought on in daily work conditions was the primary health concern. There are other researches which have named stress that is related to work is the main reason for stress in adults. In today's workplace environment where downsizing, increases in technology, and contractual employment has given rise to stress in the workplace, organizations need to be cautious about how their workers are able to tolerate stress and the effect that the stress has on the institution in general.

There are types of aggression in the workplace which can flourish in stressful times. There has been a study conducted on workplace harassment by looking at the connection between bullying behavior and stressful work environments. Workplace bullying is defined as "frequent negative actions and practices that are aimed at a person who is typically insulted, teased and who thinks for himself or herself as not possessing the recourses or the possibilities to get revenge against such behavior."

The study has proved that bullying behavior is absolutely related with weak leadership and stressful work situations in organizations. Therefore, when stress in on the increase in an institution, the propensity to behave aggressively also increases. The way a person tolerates stress or reacts to stress affects how their behavior is impacted by stress.

The measure of stress tolerance in the stress management meta-factor is the instrument for EQ-i measuring. Stress tolerance is defined as the ability to constructively and effectively handle emotions in conditions that are stressful. The said ability depends on three things: selecting actions that is positive to cope with the stress, having a disposition that is optimistic toward new experiences and change, and feeling that a person can influence or control a stressful situation.

Though the MSCEIT instruments specifically does not evaluate stress tolerance. Authors of the test have concluded that people who have high emotional intelligence are able to cope more effectively with stress due to their necessary emotional skills and have better and better regulation of their emotions. Also, there are many researchers that use the MSCEIT in order to explore employees' reaction to stress.

There have been researchers that have predicted that people who have higher EI are able to deal with stressful situations in ways that are more constructive than individuals who have lower EI.

Workplace Aggression

Workplace aggression is considered as a more specific type of aggression and it is studied widely by organizational and industrial psychologists. This type of aggression can also be referred to by different names like counterproductive behavior, workplace incivility, workplace deviance, sexual harassment, interpersonal and organizational deviance, and bullying. Nonetheless, when focusing on a nonviolent type of workplace aggression, most of the researchers refer to it as workplace deviant behaviors.

Aggressive behaviors in the workplace have been extensively studied keeping in mind aspect of the precursors or effect on the coworkers and the organization. Most of the researchers consider workplace deviant behaviors as a behavior which violates important organizational norms and threatens the well-being of the organization or its members or both.

Most of the researchers say that there is a common ground in expressing workplace aggression. There seems to be two basic general causes: organizational or situational factors and employees' individual traits. There has been a study that had examined certain situation factors – apparent organizational sanctions against violent behavior and apparent interpersonal ill-treatment – and two factors that are individual-specific -- trait aggression and trait anger – as possible precursors to workplace aggressions. It has been suggested that aggression in the workplace against colleagues has been mostly caused by individual-specific factors while violent behavior in the workplace towards the organization has been mostly caused by situations factors.

Characteristics of the social framework which are seen by workers are mostly biased by other colleagues of the institution are referred to as situational factors. When these factors are the precursors of aggression in the workplace, the acts of aggression is considered to be as a form of retaliation by the employee as reactive aggression. This means that acts of workplace aggression are reactions to situations.

Studying personality factors as cause of aggression is somewhat new in comparison with studies on other factors like gender which has been done long back in the 1950s. Most of the studies have focused on examining personality factors which may affect the degrees of aggressive behavior, both unprovoked and provoked or in situations that are neutral.

Though there have been studies that has suggested about the influence of personality factors on aggressive behaviors, both in unprovoked and provoked situations, other studies prove that personality is responsible for aggression in provoked situations only. Provided that personality does appear to have an impact on behaviors that are aggressive, researchers started to explore the impact of personality factors on patters of aggression.

It has been stated that two patterns of aggression that are influenced by personality factors: the first is the impulsive, affective dimension of aggression, and the second is the instrumental and social-cognitive dimension of aggression. However, researchers have yet to understand fully why and which personality variables can be associated with aggressive behavior.

Research has shown that personality can prejudice incoming information thus leading to behaviors that are aggressive. It has been found that people with lack of self-regulation, aggression-related cognition and negative affect acquired early in their childhood show negative bias or prejudice towards incoming information.

Managing with Emotional Intelligence

Emotional intelligence or EI is the ability to recognize one's own feelings and those of other people, to be motivated and to motivate others, and to manage one's own emotions and those of other people. EI has the following competencies:

Self-awareness

Self-management

Social awareness

Social skills

In simpler terms, EI is developed when one commits one's self to build practical competencies in daily situations.

EI: Empathy

Among of the foundation skills that lead to the success of a leader or manager is the ability to empathize. Empathy starts with awareness of the self, and in understanding one's own emotions which is critical in order to understand the emotions and feelings of other people. This is something that is extremely important for leading other people and communicating effectively.

Interpersonal problems that lead to sub-standard performance, problems with relationships with customers, and executive derailment are most commonly caused by a lack of empathy.

Emotional Competence Deficiencies

Research has found that the main causes of executive derailment consist of deficiencies on emotional competence, and the major ones are:

Inability or difficulty in handling change

Inability to work well within a group or team

Deficient interpersonal relations

When managers lack the flexibility to adapt to change, are unable to work well in a team, and are unable to relate with the people who can affect the results that they are aiming for, they are said to have inadequate capacity to comprehend other people's point of view.

Emotional Intelligence in Practice

The question is; what does EI have to do with managing and leading? Empathy denotes the foundation skill for all the important social competencies:

Sensing the feelings and perspective of others

Anticipating, meeting and recognizing the needs of customers

Sensing the development needs of other people and reinforcing their abilities

Cultivating opportunities through diversity

Reading the social and political currents in a company or organization

Leaders and managers normally possess such characteristics and traits that enable them to successfully complete tasks and projects assigned to them. It is the reason why they are then promoted to higher management positions. Their success depends on being able to focus, concentrate, and persevere.

Empathic skills involve paying adequate attention to others. They involve listening, building relationships, attending to the wants and needs of others. When a manager or leader possesses high empathic skills, they are more likely to inspire their members. Those who are able to understand people and communicate their understanding are more likely to be respected and well-liked. Thus, practicing empathy is able to improve performance. When a leader is respected, the people he or she leads will be more than likely to do their utmost to deliver better results. Focus and empathy must be balanced and once they are in equilibrium, the manager's skills become highly effective.

Employees and managers need to possess empathy in order to interact effectively with suppliers, customers, general public and with each other. Managers require it more when they are giving a task to a person or team who may not like it, when they are offering criticism, when interacting with people they do not particularly like, when facing disputes with employees and when they are delivering some unfavorable news.

ACTIVITIES

1. LIST EACH OF THE FIVE PARTS OF EMOTIONAL INTELLIGENCE

2. DESCRIBE WHY EACH OF THE FIVE PARTS ARE SO IMPORTANT

3. USE THE NEXT FEW PAGES TO DESCRIBE IN DETAIL HOW WILL YOU INCREASE EACH PART OF EMOTIONAL INTELLIGENCE. IN OTHER WORDS WHAT IS YOUR PLAN OF ACTION TO INCREASE YOUR EMOTIONAL INTELLIGENCE?